Irish Pub
COOKING

This edition published in 2010

LOVE FOOD is an imprint of Parragon Books Ltd

Parragon
Queen Street House
4 Queen Street
Bath BA1 1HE, UK

ISBN: 978-1-4075-6447-0

Printed in China

Notes for the Reader
This book uses imperial, metric, and US cup measurements. Follow the same units of measurement throughout; do not mix imperial and metric. All spoon measurements are level: teaspoons are assumed to be 5 ml, and tablespoons are assumed to be 15 ml. Unless otherwise stated, milk is assumed to be whole, eggs and individual vegetables, such as potatoes, are medium, and pepper is freshly ground black pepper.

The times given are an approximate guide only. Preparation times differ according to the techniques used by different people and the cooking times may also vary from those given as a result of the type of oven used. Optional ingredients, variations, or serving suggestions have not been included in the calculations.

Recipes using raw or very lightly cooked eggs should be avoided by infants, the elderly, pregnant women, convalescents, and anyone with a chronic condition. Pregnant and breast-feeding women are advised to avoid eating peanuts and peanut products. People with nut allergies should be aware that some of the prepared ingredients used in the recipes in this book may contain nuts. Always check the packaging before use.

Picture acknowledgments
The publisher would like to thank Getty Images for permission to reproduce copyright material: Cover (1st row center & right; 2nd row left & right; 4th row left; 5th row center) and pages 5 (center), 7, 10, 22, 27, 33, 45, 46, 51, 57, 63, 65, 71, 77, & 78.

Contents

Introduction

The traditional Irish pub has a long and venerable history. From quaint country taverns with their thatched roofs and cozy snugs to metropolitan bars with their Victorian wood paneling and patterned tiled floors, pubs in Ireland have long been places of sanctuary where people of all classes and creeds can go to forget their everyday cares, engage in lively banter, and share a beverage or two in an atmosphere of relaxed conviviality. They also play an important role in community life to the extent that, still today, some rural and market-town pubs double up as the village shop, post office, or even undertaker. Such is the appeal of the authentic Irish pub that bars in many international cities have attempted to replicate its essential charm, with varying degrees of success!

Yet there is more to the Irish pub than drinking and revelry. Today, many pubs across the Emerald Isle are popular eating establishments in their own right, serving both familiar favorites and more contemporary dishes. While it may not be possible to recreate the ambience of a traditional Irish pub in your own home, you can certainly experience a taste of Irish pub cuisine by sampling the recipes in this book. Conveniently split into four chapters that follow the course of a typical meal, this book contains all the recipes you will need to cook up an Irish-style feast. In Appetizers & Snacks, you will find a range of dishes that would be ideal for a light lunch or the first course of a more substantial meal. Entrées contains recipes for homely stews, casseroles, and pies that are guaranteed to warm you up on a cold winter's day. In Vegetables & Sides, there are a whole host of vegetable dishes, as well as breads and other savory snacks. Finally, Desserts & Drinks contains a selection of hot and cold desserts, plus a couple of drinks—the perfect way to round off any meal.

Chapter 1

APPETIZERS & SNACKS

Leek & Potato Soup

Leeks and potatoes are staples in Irish cuisine. For cooking, small, tender leeks are better than huge ones. This soup can be roughly blended to give a hearty, country texture or blended until smooth and served with cream and snipped chives for a more luxurious soup.

Serves 4–6

4 tbsp butter
1 onion, chopped
3 leeks, sliced
2 potatoes, cut into $^3/_4$-inch/2-cm cubes
$3^1/_2$ cups vegetable stock
salt and pepper
$^2/_3$ cup light cream, to serve (optional)
2 tbsp snipped fresh chives,
  to garnish

- Melt the butter in a large saucepan over medium heat, add the onion, leeks, and potatoes, and sauté gently for 2–3 minutes, until soft but not brown. Pour in the stock, bring to a boil, then reduce the heat and simmer, covered, for 15 minutes.

- Transfer the mixture to a food processor or blender and process until smooth. Return to the rinsed-out saucepan.

- Reheat the soup and season to taste with salt and pepper. Ladle into warmed bowls and serve, swirled with the cream, if using, and garnished with the chives.

Smoked Cod Chowder

With its hundreds of miles of coastline, it is no wonder that Ireland is famous for its fabulous fish and seafood. This recipe uses smoked cod, which gives the chowder a wonderfully rich flavor. Use undyed fillets if you can find them.

Serves 4

2 tbsp butter
1 onion, finely chopped
1 small celery stalk, finely diced
2 potatoes, diced
1 carrot, diced
1¼ cups boiling water
12 oz/350 g smoked cod fillets, skinned and cut into bite-size pieces
1¼ cups milk
salt and pepper
fresh flat-leaf parsley sprigs, to garnish

Melt the butter in a large pan over low heat, add the onion and celery, and cook, stirring frequently, for 5 minutes, or until softened but not browned.

Add the potatoes, carrot, water, and salt and pepper to taste. Bring to a boil, then reduce the heat and let simmer for 10 minutes, or until the vegetables are tender. Add the fish to the chowder and cook for an additional 10 minutes.

Pour in the milk and heat gently. Taste and adjust the seasoning, adding salt and pepper to taste. Serve hot, garnished with parsley sprigs.

MUSSENDEN TEMPLE, COUNTY DERRY

Split Pea & Ham Soup

This heartwarming soup benefits from the long, slow cooking process used in this recipe. It is a great way to use up any leftover ham and is perfect on its own as a light lunch or served with bread for a filling and satisfying main meal.

Serves 6–8

$2^{1}/_{2}$ cups split green peas
1 tbsp olive oil
1 large onion, finely chopped
1 large carrot, finely chopped
1 celery stalk, finely chopped
4 cups chicken or vegetable stock
4 cups water
8 oz/225 g lean smoked ham, finely diced
$^{1}/_{4}$ tsp dried thyme
$^{1}/_{4}$ tsp dried marjoram
1 bay leaf
salt and pepper

- Rinse the peas under cold running water. Put in a saucepan and cover generously with water. Bring to a boil and boil for 3 minutes, skimming off the foam from the surface. Drain the peas.

- Heat the oil in a large saucepan over medium heat. Add the onion and cook for 3–4 minutes, stirring occasionally, until just softened.

- Add the carrot and celery and continue cooking for 2 minutes. Add the peas, pour over the stock and water, and stir to combine.

- Bring just to a boil and stir the ham into the soup. Add the thyme, marjoram, and bay leaf. Reduce the heat, cover, and cook gently for $1–1^{1}/_{2}$ hours, until the ingredients are very soft. Remove the bay leaf.

- Taste and adjust the seasoning, adding salt and pepper to taste. Ladle into warmed soup bowls and serve.

Rye Toast with Roast Beef & Coleslaw

Beef and cabbage is a classic and very tasty combination, as demonstrated by this chunky beef sandwich with homemade coleslaw. You can use any leftover corned beef (see page 28) in place of the roast beef.

Serves 1

- 1 tbsp finely chopped fresh ginger or horseradish sauce
- $1\frac{1}{2}$ tbsp butter, softened
- 2 slices light rye bread, preferably with caraway seeds
- 1 very thin slice white or green cabbage
- 1 small carrot, coarsely shredded
- 1 scallion, sliced
- 1 large slice roast beef
- salt and pepper
- dill pickles, to serve (optional)

Preheat a sandwich toaster, the broiler, or a griddle. Mix the ginger with the butter.

Spread one slice of bread generously with some of the butter. Top with the cabbage, trimming any overhanging shreds and placing them back on the middle of the sandwich. Top with the carrot and scallion, keeping them away from the edge. Season lightly with salt and pepper.

Spread a little more of the butter on one side of the beef and lay it, butter side down, on the carrot. Spread the remaining butter on the second slice of bread and place it on top of the sandwich, butter side down.

Toast the sandwich in the toaster, under the broiler (well away from the heat), or on a griddle until crisp and golden. Turn it over once when cooking under the broiler or on the griddle to cook both sides. Serve immediately with dill pickles, if using.

Glazed Beet & Egg Sourdough Toasts

With their vibrant color and sweet flavor, beets look just as good as they taste. In this recipe, they are partnered with chopped boiled eggs to make a tasty toast topping. When cooking fresh beets, leave 1 inch/2.5 cm of stem attached to prevent the color from "bleeding" and peel after cooking.

Serves 2–4

4 eggs
1 lb 2 oz/500 g cooked beets
  (fresh or vacuum-packed
  without vinegar)
2 tsp sugar
5 tsp apple cider vinegar
4 slices sourdough bread
6 tbsp olive oil
1 tbsp Dijon mustard
3 tbsp chopped fresh dill
salt and pepper

❧ Preheat the broiler to medium–high. Cook the eggs in a pan of boiling water for 8 minutes, then drain, peel, and chop them. Set aside. Dice the beets quite small and place in a small bowl. Mix in half the sugar and 1 teaspoon of the vinegar and season to taste with salt and pepper.

❧ Brush the bread with a little of the oil and toast under the preheated broiler for 2–3 minutes, until crisp and golden.

❧ Meanwhile, drizzle 1 teaspoon of the remaining oil over the beets. Whisk together the remaining vinegar and sugar with the mustard and salt and pepper to taste. Gradually whisk in the remaining oil to make a thick dressing. Stir in the dill and taste for seasoning—it should be sweet and mustardy, with a sharpness—add more sugar or vinegar if you like.

❧ Stir the beets, then turn the bread over and cover the slices with the beets right up to the crusts. Glaze the beets under the broiler for 2–3 minutes, until browned in places.

❧ Cut the bread slices in halves or quarters and top with the chopped egg. Drizzle with a little dressing and serve immediately.

Bleu Cheese & Walnut Tartlets

So lush and green are the pasture lands that Irish dairy herds graze upon that it is no surprise that the resulting cheeses are of equally fine quality. Try using an Irish bleu cheese, such as Cashel Blue, to make these tartlets. Many Irish cheeses are available worldwide in specialty stores and larger supermarkets.

Makes 12

Pie Dough

1¹/₂ cups all-purpose flour, plus extra
  for dusting
pinch of celery salt
scant ¹/₂ cup cold butter, cut into pieces,
  plus extra for greasing
¹/₄ cup walnut halves, finely chopped

Filling

2 tbsp butter
2 celery stalks, trimmed and finely
  chopped
1 small leek, trimmed and finely
  chopped
scant 1 cup heavy cream,
  plus 2 tbsp extra
7 oz/200 g bleu cheese
3 egg yolks
salt and pepper

❧ Lightly grease twelve 3-inch/7.5-cm holes in a muffin pan. Sift the flour and celery salt into a food processor, add the butter, and process until the mixture resembles fine breadcrumbs. Transfer the mixture to a bowl and add the walnuts and a little cold water, just enough to bring the dough together.

❧ Turn out onto a floured counter and cut the dough in half. Roll out the first piece and cut out six 3¹/₂-inch/9-cm circles. Take each circle and roll out to 4¹/₂ inches/12 cm in diameter and fit into the muffin holes, pressing to fill the holes. Do the same with the remaining dough. Put a piece of parchment paper in each hole, fill with dried beans, and let chill in the refrigerator for 30 minutes. Meanwhile, preheat the oven to 400°F/200°C.

❧ Remove the muffin pan from the refrigerator and bake the tartlets blind in the preheated oven for 10 minutes, then carefully remove the paper and beans.

❧ Melt the butter in a skillet, add the celery and leek, and cook for 15 minutes, until soft. Add the 2 tablespoons of cream and crumble in the bleu cheese. Mix well and season to taste with salt and pepper. Bring the remaining cream to a simmer in a separate pan, then pour onto the egg yolks, stirring all the time. Mix in the bleu cheese mixture and spoon into the pastry shells. Bake for 10 minutes, then turn the pan around in the oven and bake for an additional 5 minutes. Let cool in the pan for 5 minutes before serving.

Smoked Salmon, Dill & Horseradish Tartlets

Salmon has been smoked in Ireland for many centuries, using traditional smoking techniques that capture and enhance both the flavor and texture of this fantastic fish. If you're short of time, you can use store-bought flaky pie dough in this recipe.

Makes 6

Pie Dough
heaping ¾ cup all-purpose flour, plus extra for dusting
pinch of salt
5 tbsp cold butter, cut into pieces, plus extra for greasing

Filling
½ cup sour cream
1 tsp creamed horseradish
½ tsp lemon juice
1 tsp Spanish capers, chopped
3 egg yolks
7 oz/200 g smoked salmon trimmings
bunch of fresh dill, chopped, plus extra sprigs to garnish
salt and pepper

❅ Grease six 3½-inch/9-cm loose-bottom tartlet pans. Sift the flour and salt into a food processor, add the butter, and process until the mixture resembles fine breadcrumbs. Transfer the mixture to a large bowl and add a little cold water, just enough to bring the dough together.

❅ Turn out onto a floured counter and divide into 6 equal-size pieces. Roll each piece to fit the tartlet pans. Carefully fit each piece of dough in its shell and press well to fit the pan. Roll the rolling pin over the pan to neaten the edges and trim the excess dough. Put a piece of parchment paper in each pan, fill with dried beans, and let chill in the refrigerator for 30 minutes. Meanwhile, preheat the oven to 400°F/200°C.

❅ Bake the tartlet shells blind in the preheated oven for 10 minutes, then carefully remove the paper and beans.

❅ Meanwhile, put the sour cream, horseradish, lemon juice, and capers into a bowl with salt and pepper to taste and mix well. Add the egg yolks, smoked salmon, and chopped dill and carefully mix again. Divide this mixture among the tartlet shells and return to the oven for 10 minutes. Let cool in the pans for 5 minutes before serving, garnished with dill sprigs.

Garlic & Herb Dublin Bay Prawns

Dublin Bay prawns are part of the lobster family and are also known as langoustines or scampi. Fresh Dublin Bay prawns are available outside Ireland, but if you can't find them, you can use jumbo shrimp instead. This dish is delicious served with a glass of chilled white wine.

Serves 2

12 raw Dublin Bay prawns or jumbo
   shrimp in their shells
juice of 1/2 lemon
2 garlic cloves, crushed
3 tbsp chopped fresh parsley
1 tbsp chopped fresh dill
3 tbsp butter, softened
salt and pepper
lemon wedges and crusty bread,
   to serve

❖ Rinse the prawns. Devein, using a sharp knife to slice along the back from the head end to the tail and removing the thin black intestine.

❖ Mix the lemon juice with the garlic, herbs, and butter to form a paste. Season well with salt and pepper. Spread the paste over the prawns and let marinate for 30 minutes.

❖ Preheat the broiler to medium. Cook the prawns under the preheated broiler for 5–6 minutes. Alternatively, heat a skillet and fry the prawns until cooked. Turn out onto warmed plates and pour over the pan juices. Serve immediately with lemon wedges and crusty bread.

DUNLUCE CASTLE, COUNTY ANTRIM

Potted Crab

"Potting" is a method from pre-refrigeration days for preserving all kinds of meat and fish. More recently, it has become a way of stretching extravagant ingredients a little further. The food is packed into small pots and covered with a layer of melted butter or other fat to exclude the air.

Serves 4–6

1 large cooked crab, prepared by your
   fish dealer if possible
whole nutmeg, for grating
2 pinches of cayenne pepper or mace
juice of 1 lemon
1 cup lightly salted butter
salt and pepper
buttered toast, to serve

✤ If the crab is not already prepared, pick out all the meat, being careful to remove all the meat from the claws.

✤ Mix together the white and brown meat but do not mash too smoothly. Season well with salt and pepper and add a good grating of nutmeg and the cayenne pepper. Add the lemon juice to taste. Melt half the butter in a saucepan and carefully mix in the crabmeat. Turn the mixture out into 4–6 small soufflé dishes or ramekins.

✤ In a clean saucepan, heat the remaining butter until it melts, then continue heating for a few moments until it stops bubbling. Let the sediment settle and carefully pour the clarified butter over the crab mixture. This seal of clarified butter will let you keep the potted crab for 1–2 days. Chill in the refrigerator for 1–2 hours.

✤ Serve with plenty of buttered toast.

Chapter 2
ENTRÉES

Corned Beef & Cabbage

This dish is traditionally eaten in the United States to celebrate Saint Patrick's Day. In the past, the brining liquid may have included saltpeter, a bactericide that also produces the characteristic pink color. Saltpeter is no longer available to the general public, but you may be able to buy commercial brine mix from a good butcher.

Serves 6–8

16 cups water
1 lb 9 oz/700 g coarse salt or brine mix
3 lb 5 oz/1.5 kg brisket or beef round
12 black peppercorns
4 cloves
3 bay leaves
1 large onion, sliced
6 carrots, cut into chunks
1 turnip, thickly sliced
6 large potatoes, cut into chunks
1 savoy or green cabbage, cored and
  cut into wedges
2 tbsp chopped fresh parsley
mustard, to serve

❖ Pour the water into a large plastic or ceramic container and chill in the refrigerator for 1 hour. Stir in the salt until it has dissolved completely, then add the meat, making sure that it is completely submerged.

❖ Put the container in the refrigerator and let stand for 7–10 days. Check daily that the meat is still submerged and skim off any foam that rises to the surface.

❖ Drain the meat, discarding the soaking liquid, then rinse. Put the meat into a large pan, add the peppercorns, cloves, and bay leaves, and pour in enough water to cover. Bring to a boil, skimming off any foam that rises to the surface. Reduce the heat, cover, and simmer gently for 1³/₄ hours.

❖ Add the onion, carrots, turnip, and potatoes to the pan, re-cover, and simmer for 30 minutes. Add the cabbage and parsley, re-cover, and simmer for an additional 15–30 minutes, until the meat is tender.

❖ Remove the beef, cover with aluminum foil, and let stand for 10 minutes to firm up. Strain the vegetables and put them into a warmed serving dish, discarding the peppercorns, cloves, and bay leaves. Carve the meat into slices and serve immediately with the vegetables, accompanied by mustard.

Beef in Stout with Herb Dumplings

Stout is a strong, dark beer that originated in the British Isles. The most famous Irish stout is Guinness, which is made from roasted, malted barley, hops, yeast, and water. In this hearty stew, topped with light and fluffy suet dumplings, tender chunks of slow-cooked beef are enveloped in a rich gravy.

Serves 6

Stew

2 tbsp corn oil
2 large onions, thinly sliced
8 carrots, sliced
4 tbsp all-purpose flour
2 lb 12 oz/1.25 kg braising beef,
   cut into cubes
generous 1³/₄ cups stout
2 tsp brown sugar
2 bay leaves
1 tbsp chopped fresh thyme
salt and pepper

Herb Dumplings

generous ³/₄ cup self-rising flour
pinch of salt
¹/₂ cup shredded suet
2 tbsp chopped fresh parsley, plus
   extra to garnish
about 4 tbsp water

❖ Preheat the oven to 325°F/160°C. Heat the oil in a flameproof casserole. Add the onions and carrots and cook over low heat, stirring occasionally, for 5 minutes, or until the onions are softened. Meanwhile, place the flour in a plastic bag and season well with salt and pepper. Add the beef to the bag, tie the top, and shake well to coat. Do this in batches, if necessary.

❖ Remove the vegetables from the casserole with a slotted spoon and reserve. Add the beef to the casserole, in batches, and cook, stirring frequently, until browned all over. Return all the meat and the onions and carrots to the casserole and sprinkle in any remaining seasoned flour. Pour in the stout and add the sugar, bay leaves, and thyme. Bring to a boil, cover, and cook in the preheated oven for 1³/₄ hours.

❖ To make the herb dumplings, sift the flour and salt into a bowl. Stir in the suet and parsley and add enough of the water to make a soft dough. Shape into small balls between the palms of your hands. Add to the casserole and return to the oven for 30 minutes. Remove and discard the bay leaves and serve, sprinkled with parsley.

Irish Stew

This robust stew was traditionally made using lamb or mutton (meat from a sheep over 1 year old), potatoes, onions, and sometimes carrots. It is a white stew, meaning that the meat is not browned. If you have time, make it a day in advance because this will let the delicious flavors blend together.

Serves 4

4 tbsp all-purpose flour
3 lb/1.3 kg middle neck of lamb,
  trimmed of visible fat
3 large onions, chopped
3 carrots, sliced
1 lb/450 g potatoes, cut into quarters
$\frac{1}{2}$ tsp dried thyme
scant $3\frac{1}{2}$ cups hot beef stock
salt and pepper
2 tbsp chopped fresh parsley,
  to garnish

❧ Preheat the oven to 325°F/160°C. Place the flour in a plastic bag and season well with salt and pepper. Add the lamb to the bag, tie the top, and shake well to coat. Do this in batches, if necessary. Arrange in the bottom of a casserole.

❧ Layer the onions, carrots, and potatoes on top of the lamb.

❧ Sprinkle in the thyme and pour in the stock, then cover and cook in the preheated oven for $2\frac{1}{2}$ hours. Garnish with the chopped parsley and serve straight from the casserole.

HALFPENNY BRIDGE, DUBLIN

Pot-Roast Pork

Pork has long been a popular meat in Ireland. In this tasty dish, tender pork loin is slowly braised in hard cider and stock. The resulting cooking liquid is then enriched with cream to create a delicious sauce.

Serves 4

1 tbsp corn oil
4 tbsp butter
2 lb 4 oz/1 kg boned and rolled pork loin
4 shallots, chopped
6 juniper berries
2 fresh thyme sprigs, plus extra to garnish
$^{2}/_{3}$ cup hard cider
$^{2}/_{3}$ cup chicken stock or water
8 celery stalks, chopped
2 tbsp all-purpose flour
$^{2}/_{3}$ cup heavy cream
salt and pepper
freshly cooked peas, to serve

- Heat the oil with half the butter in a heavy-bottom pan or flameproof casserole. Add the pork and cook over medium heat, turning frequently, for 5–10 minutes, or until browned. Transfer to a plate.

- Add the shallots to the pan and cook, stirring frequently, for 5 minutes, or until softened. Add the juniper berries and thyme sprigs and return the pork to the pan, with any juices that have collected on the plate. Pour in the cider and stock, season to taste with salt and pepper, then cover and simmer for 30 minutes. Turn the pork over and add the celery. Re-cover the pan and cook for an additional 40 minutes.

- Meanwhile, make a beurre manié by mashing the remaining butter with the flour in a small bowl. Transfer the pork and celery to a platter with a slotted spoon and keep warm. Remove and discard the juniper berries and thyme. Whisk the beurre manié, a little at a time, into the simmering cooking liquid. Cook, stirring constantly, for 2 minutes, then stir in the cream and bring to a boil.

- Slice the pork and spoon a little of the sauce over it. Garnish with thyme sprigs and serve immediately with the celery, peas, and the remaining sauce.

Potato, Leek & Chicken Pie

The humble pie is a mainstay of Irish cuisine, being as versatile as it is delicious. This modern take on the traditional chicken and leek pie uses filo pastry to give it a crispy topping. Unlike many pies, it is the perfect dish for a summer's day because it is light and not at all stodgy.

Serves 4

2 waxy potatoes, cubed
1/2 cup butter
1 skinless chicken breast fillet, about
  6 oz/175 g, cubed
1 leek, sliced
generous 1 1/2 cups sliced chestnut
  mushrooms
2 1/2 tbsp all-purpose flour
1 1/4 cups milk
1 tbsp Dijon mustard
2 tbsp chopped fresh sage
8 oz/225 g store-bought filo pastry,
  thawed if frozen
salt and pepper

❇ Preheat the oven to 350°F/180°C. Cook the potatoes in a pan of boiling water for 5 minutes. Drain and set aside.

❇ Melt 5 tablespoons of the butter in a skillet and cook the chicken for 5 minutes, or until browned all over.

❇ Add the leek and mushrooms and cook for 3 minutes, stirring. Stir in the flour and cook for 1 minute, stirring constantly. Gradually stir in the milk and bring to a boil. Add the mustard, sage, and potatoes, season to taste with salt and pepper, and simmer for 10 minutes.

❇ Meanwhile, melt the remaining butter in a small pan. Line a deep pie dish with half of the sheets of filo pastry. Spoon the chicken mixture into the dish and cover with 1 sheet of pastry. Brush the pastry with melted butter and lay another sheet on top. Brush this sheet with butter.

❇ Cut the remaining filo pastry into strips and fold them onto the top of the pie to create a ruffled effect. Brush the strips with the melted butter and cook in the preheated oven for 45 minutes, or until golden brown and crisp. Serve hot.

Fisherman's Pie

Fish pie is a popular everyday comfort food, and it can be a very fine dish when made with good-quality, fresh ingredients. The rich, creamy sauce and the addition of shrimp and fresh herbs add to the luxury feel, making this a dish worthy of gracing any table.

Serves 6

2 lb/900 g whitefish fillets, skinned
2/3 cup dry white wine
1 tbsp chopped fresh parsley, tarragon, or dill
1 1/4 cups sliced mushrooms
scant 1/2 cup butter, plus extra for greasing
6 oz/175 g cooked peeled shrimp
1/4 cup all-purpose flour
1/2 cup heavy cream
2 lb/900 g starchy potatoes
salt and pepper

❧ Preheat the oven to 350°F/180°C. Grease a 7 1/2-cup baking dish.

❧ Place the fish fillets in the baking dish. Season well with salt and pepper, pour over the wine, and scatter over the parsley.

❧ Cover with foil and bake in the preheated oven for 15 minutes, until the flesh starts to flake. Strain off the cooking liquid and reserve for the sauce. Increase the oven temperature to 425°F/220°C.

❧ Cook the mushrooms in a skillet with 1 tablespoon of the butter, then spoon over the fish. Scatter over the shrimp.

❧ Heat 4 tablespoons of the remaining butter in a pan and stir in the flour. Cook for a few minutes without browning, then remove from the heat and add the reserved cooking liquid, stirring well between additions.

❧ Return to the heat and gently bring to a boil, stirring to ensure a smooth sauce. Add the cream and season to taste with salt and pepper. Pour over the fish mixture and smooth over the surface.

❧ Meanwhile, cook the potatoes in a large pan of boiling salted water for 15–20 minutes. Drain well and mash with a potato masher until smooth. Season to taste with salt and pepper and add the remaining butter, stirring until melted.

❧ Spoon the mashed potatoes on top of the fish mixture and sauce and smooth the surface to cover completely. Bake for 10–15 minutes, until golden brown.

Fish Cakes

Homemade fish cakes are a popular offering in seaside pubs, and their flavor is in a completely different league to that of the bland frozen fish cakes you may have eaten as a child. You can vary the fish according to what is available—a mixture of fresh and smoked fish would provide a sophisticated touch.

Serves 4

1 lb/450 g starchy potatoes, peeled
   and cut into chunks
1 lb/450 g mixed fish fillets, such as
   cod and salmon, skinned
2 tbsp chopped fresh tarragon
grated rind of 1 lemon
2 tbsp heavy cream
1 tbsp all-purpose flour
1 egg, beaten
2 cups fresh breadcrumbs
4 tbsp vegetable oil, for frying
salt and pepper
arugula and lemon wedges, to serve

- Cook the potatoes in a large pan of boiling salted water for 15–20 minutes. Drain well and mash with a potato masher until smooth.

- Place the fish in a skillet and just cover with water. Place over medium heat and bring to a boil, then reduce the heat, cover, and simmer gently for 5 minutes, until cooked.

- Remove from the heat and drain the fish onto a plate. When cool enough to handle, flake the fish into large chunks, ensuring that there are no bones.

- Mix the potatoes with the fish, tarragon, lemon rind, and cream. Season well with salt and pepper and shape into 4 large patties or 8 smaller ones.

- Dust the patties with flour and dip them into the beaten egg. Coat thoroughly in the breadcrumbs. Place on a baking sheet and let chill in the refrigerator for at least 30 minutes.

- Heat the oil in a skillet and fry the patties over medium heat for 5 minutes on each side, turning them carefully using a palette knife or a spatula.

- Serve with arugula and lemon wedges for squeezing over the fish cakes.

Winter Vegetable Cobbler

While in the United States a cobbler is usually a fruit dessert, any cobbler dish found on the menu in an Irish pub is more likely to be savory rather than sweet. Cobblers are typically meat stews topped with thick circles of biscuit dough, with each circle forming a separate "cobble." This is a vegetarian version.

Serves 4

1 tbsp olive oil
1 garlic clove, crushed
8 small onions, halved
2 celery stalks, sliced
8 oz/225 g rutabaga, chopped
2 carrots, sliced
1/2 small head of cauliflower, broken
   into florets
3 1/4 cups sliced mushrooms
14 oz/400 g canned chopped tomatoes
1/4 cup red lentils, rinsed
2 tbsp cornstarch
3–4 tbsp water
1 1/4 cups vegetable stock
2 tsp Tabasco sauce
2 tsp chopped fresh oregano, plus extra
   sprigs to garnish

Cobbler Topping

2 cups self-rising flour
pinch of salt
4 tbsp butter
1 cup grated sharp cheddar cheese
2 tsp chopped fresh oregano
1 egg, lightly beaten
2/3 cup milk

Preheat the oven to 350°F/180°C. Heat the oil in a large flameproof casserole and cook the garlic and onions for 5 minutes. Add the celery, rutabaga, carrots, and cauliflower and cook for 2–3 minutes. Add the mushrooms, tomatoes, and lentils. Mix together the cornstarch and water and stir into the casserole with the stock, Tabasco, and oregano.

Cover the casserole, then transfer to the preheated oven and bake for 20 minutes.

To make the cobbler topping, sift the flour and salt into a bowl. Rub in the butter with your fingertips, then stir in most of the cheese and the oregano. Beat the egg with the milk and add enough to the dry ingredients to make a soft dough. Knead lightly, roll out to a thickness of 1/2 inch/1 cm, and cut into 2-inch/5-cm circles.

Remove the casserole from the oven and increase the oven temperature to 400°F/200°C. Arrange the biscuits around the edge of the casserole, brush with the remaining egg and milk, and sprinkle with the remaining cheese. Cook for an additional 10–12 minutes, or until the topping is golden brown. Garnish with oregano sprigs and serve.

Chapter 3

VEGETABLES & SIDES

Colcannon

Colcannon is a traditional Irish dish often served at Halloween. In some families, the cook will hide lucky charms or coins in the mixture—these are said to bring the recipients good luck or fortune. This version uses cabbage and scallions, but you can use kale and leeks instead if you prefer.

Serves 4

1 lb/450 g starchy potatoes
4 tbsp butter
²/₃ cup light cream
¹/₂ small head of green or white cabbage
6 scallions, cut into ¹/₄-inch/5-mm slices
salt and pepper

- Cook the potatoes in a large pan of boiling salted water for 15–20 minutes. Drain well and mash with a potato masher until smooth. Season to taste with salt and pepper, add the butter and cream, and stir well.

- Cut the cabbage in half, remove and discard the central stalk, and shred finely. Cook the cabbage in a large pan of boiling salted water for 1–2 minutes, until it is soft. Drain thoroughly.

- Mix the cabbage and mashed potatoes together, then stir in the scallions. Season well with salt and pepper.

- Serve immediately in individual bowls.

THATCHED COTTAGES, COUNTY WATERFORD

Potato Cakes

Potato cakes used to be a way of using up leftover potatoes, but it is worth making some fresh mashed potatoes for this recipe because this makes the cakes particularly light and tasty. They are delicious served hot and smothered with butter.

Serves 4

1 lb 4 oz/ 550 g starchy potatoes, cut into chunks
2 tbsp butter, plus extra to serve
1 egg (optional)
generous 3/4 cup all-purpose flour, plus extra for dusting
oil, for brushing
salt and pepper

❖ Cook the potatoes in a large pan of boiling salted water for 15–20 minutes. Drain well and mash with a potato masher until smooth. Season to taste with salt and pepper and add the butter. Mix in the egg, if using.

❖ Turn out into a large mixing bowl and add enough of the flour to make a light dough. Work quickly because you do not want the potatoes to cool too much.

❖ Place the dough on a lightly floured counter and roll out carefully to a thickness of 1/4 inch/5 mm. Using a 2 1/2-inch/6-cm cookie cutter, cut into circles.

❖ Brush a flat grill pan or heavy-bottom skillet with oil and heat. Cook the potato cakes in batches in the grill pan for 4–5 minutes on each side, until golden brown.

❖ Serve immediately with butter.

Glazed Turnips

Ireland's wet climate makes it the perfect place to grow turnips. This much underrated root vegetable is best picked while still small, when the flavor is delicate and slightly sweet. The taste gets stronger as turnips age and the texture becomes coarser, sometimes woody.

Serves 4–6

2 lb/900 g young turnips, peeled and
  quartered
4 tbsp butter
1 tbsp brown sugar
$^2/_3$ cup vegetable stock
1 sprig of fresh rosemary
salt and pepper
chopped fresh parsley and grated
  orange rind, to garnish

❄ Put the turnips into a large pan of boiling salted water, bring back to a boil, and simmer for 10 minutes. Drain well.

❄ Melt the butter in the rinsed-out pan over low heat, add the turnips and sugar, and mix to coat well.

❄ Add the stock with the rosemary and bring to a boil. Reduce the heat and simmer for 15–20 minutes with the lid off the pan so that the juices reduce and the turnips are tender and well glazed.

❄ Remove the pan from the heat, discard the rosemary, and season to taste with salt and pepper.

❄ Serve immediately garnished with parsley and orange rind.

BOTANIC GARDENS, BELFAST

Sweet & Sour Red Cabbage

Cabbage is a vegetable that is particularly associated with Ireland, although it is only in the last century that so many different varieties have been available. In this tasty recipe, red cabbage is cooked with apples and flavored with spices.

Serves 6–8

1 medium head of red cabbage
2 tbsp olive oil
2 onions, finely sliced
1 garlic clove, chopped
2 small baking apples, peeled, cored, and sliced
2 tbsp light brown sugar
½ tsp ground cinnamon
1 tsp crushed juniper berries
whole nutmeg, for grating
2 tbsp red wine vinegar
grated rind and juice of 1 orange
2 tbsp cranberry jelly
salt and pepper

❖ Cut the cabbage into quarters, remove and discard the central stalk, and shred finely.

❖ Heat the oil in a large pan and add the cabbage, onions, garlic, and apples. Sprinkle over the sugar, cinnamon, and juniper berries and grate a quarter of the nutmeg into the pan.

❖ Pour over the vinegar and orange juice and add the orange rind. Stir well and season to taste with salt and pepper.

❖ Cook over medium heat, stirring occasionally, until the cabbage is just tender but still has "bite." This will take 10–15 minutes, depending on how finely the cabbage is sliced.

❖ Stir in the cranberry jelly and add more salt and pepper if necessary. Serve hot.

Honeyed Parsnips

In this recipe, oven roasting brings out the natural sweetness of the parsnips, which is then further enhanced by the addition of honey. These parsnips are the perfect accompaniment to any kind of roast meat.

Serves 4

8 parsnips, peeled and cut into quarters
4 tbsp vegetable oil
1 tbsp honey

❖ Preheat the oven to 350°F/180°C.

❖ Bring a large pan of water to a boil. Reduce the heat, add the parsnips, and cook for 5 minutes. Drain thoroughly.

❖ Pour 2 tablespoons of the oil into a shallow, ovenproof dish and add the parsnips. Mix the remaining oil with the honey and drizzle over the parsnips. Roast in the preheated oven for 45 minutes, until golden brown and tender. Remove from the oven and serve.

Irish Soda Bread

Soda bread has long been a staple in Ireland. It is a bread made without yeast, the leavening agent being baking soda mixed with buttermilk. A cross is cut into the top of the bread to help it rise and, according to Irish folklore, to either ward off evil or to let the fairies out.

Makes 1 loaf

vegetable oil, for brushing
4 cups all-purpose flour, plus extra
  for dusting
1 tsp salt
1 tsp baking soda
1³/₄ cups buttermilk

❇ Preheat the oven to 425°F/220°C. Brush a baking sheet with oil.

❇ Sift the flour, salt, and baking soda into a bowl. Make a well in the center and pour in most of the buttermilk. Mix well, first with a wooden spoon and then with your hands. The dough should be very soft but not too wet. If necessary, add the remaining buttermilk.

❇ Turn out the dough onto a lightly floured counter and knead lightly and briefly. Shape into an 8-inch/20-cm round. Put the loaf onto the prepared baking sheet and cut a cross in the top with a sharp knife.

❇ Bake in the preheated oven for 25–30 minutes, until golden brown and the loaf sounds hollow when tapped on the bottom. Transfer to a wire rack and let cool slightly. Serve warm.

TRIM CASTLE, COUNTY MEATH

Oatmeal & Potato Bread

This recipe uses freshly cooked potatoes, but it is also a wonderful way to use up leftover mashed potatoes. It makes a dense, moist loaf that is the perfect accompaniment to any meal, although it is particularly delicious served with a traditional Irish fried breakfast.

Makes 1 loaf

oil, for oiling
2 mealy potatoes
3$\frac{1}{2}$ cups white bread flour,
  plus extra for dusting
1$\frac{1}{2}$ tsp salt
3 tbsp butter, diced
1$\frac{1}{2}$ tsp active dry yeast
1$\frac{1}{2}$ tbsp dark brown sugar
3 tbsp rolled oats
2 tbsp skim milk powder
scant 1 cup lukewarm water

Topping
1 tbsp water
1 tbsp rolled oats

❇ Oil a 9 x 5 x 3-inch/23 x 13 x 8-cm loaf pan. Put the potatoes in a large pan, add water to cover, and bring to a boil. Cook for 20–25 minutes, until tender. Drain, then mash until smooth. Let cool.

❇ Sift the flour and salt into a warmed bowl. Rub in the butter with your fingertips. Stir in the yeast, sugar, oats, and milk powder. Mix in the mashed potato, then add the water and mix to a soft dough.

❇ Turn out the dough onto a lightly floured counter and knead for 5–10 minutes, or until smooth and elastic. Put the dough in an oiled bowl, cover with plastic wrap, and let rise in a warm place for 1 hour, or until doubled in size.

❇ Turn out the dough again and knead lightly. Shape into a loaf and transfer to the prepared pan. Cover and let rise in a warm place for 30 minutes. Meanwhile, preheat the oven to 425°F/220°C.

❇ Brush the surface of the loaf with the water and carefully sprinkle over the oats. Bake in the preheated oven for 25–30 minutes, or until it sounds hollow when tapped on the bottom. Transfer to a wire rack and let cool slightly. Serve warm.

Barm Brack

Barm Brack is a yeast bread with added golden raisins and raisins—it is sweeter than standard bread but not as rich as cake. It is traditionally eaten around Halloween, when charms are baked into the dough as part of an ancient fortune-telling ritual.

Makes 1 loaf

5²/₃ cups white bread flour, plus extra for dusting
1 tsp allspice
1 tsp salt
2 tsp active dry yeast
1 tbsp superfine sugar
1¹/₄ cups lukewarm milk
²/₃ cup lukewarm water
oil, for oiling
4 tbsp butter, softened, plus extra to serve
2 cups mixed dried fruit (golden raisins, currants, and raisins)
milk, for glazing

❖ Sift the flour, allspice, and salt into a warmed bowl. Stir in the yeast and superfine sugar. Make a well in the center and pour in the milk and water. Mix well to make a sticky dough. Turn the dough out onto a lightly floured counter and knead until no longer sticky. Put the dough in an oiled bowl, cover with plastic wrap, and let rise in a warm place for 1 hour, until doubled in size.

❖ Turn the dough out onto a floured counter and knead lightly for 1 minute. Add the butter and mixed fruits to the dough and work them in until completely incorporated. Return the dough to the bowl, replace the plastic wrap, and let rise for 30 minutes.

❖ Oil a 9-inch/23-cm round cake pan. Pat the dough to a neat round and fit in the pan. Cover and let rise in a warm place until it has risen to the top of the pan. Meanwhile, preheat the oven to 400°F/200°C.

❖ Brush the top of the loaf lightly with milk and bake in the preheated oven for 15 minutes. Cover the loaf with foil, reduce the oven temperature to 350°F/180°C, and bake for an additional 45 minutes, until the bread is golden and sounds hollow when tapped on the bottom. Transfer to a wire rack and let cool. Serve warm or cold with butter.

Savory Oat Crackers

These crunchy oat crackers, with added walnuts and sesame seeds, are quick and easy to make. They would be the ideal accompaniment for a cheese board—make sure to include a range of Irish cheeses and some pickles or chutney.

Makes 12–14

scant ½ cup unsalted butter, plus extra for greasing
scant 1 cup rolled oats
¼ cup whole wheat flour
½ tsp coarse salt
1 tsp dried thyme
⅓ cup walnuts, finely chopped
1 egg, beaten
3 tbsp sesame seeds

❁ Preheat the oven to 350°F/180°C. Lightly grease two baking sheets.

❁ Rub the butter into the oats and flour using your fingertips. Stir in the salt, thyme, and walnuts, then add the egg and mix to a soft dough. Break off walnut-size pieces of dough and roll into balls, then roll in sesame seeds to coat lightly and evenly.

❁ Place the balls of dough on the prepared baking sheets, spacing them well apart, and roll the rolling pin over them to flatten as much as possible. Bake in the preheated oven for 12–15 minutes, or until firm and pale golden in color.

❁ Let cool on the baking sheets for 3-4 minutes, then transfer to a wire rack to finish cooling.

GIANT'S CAUSEWAY, COUNTY ANTRIM

Chapter 4

DESSERTS & DRINKS

Bread & Butter Pudding

Warming and comforting, bread and butter pudding is the perfect dessert for a cold winter's day. It was traditionally made with dry leftover bread, but this luxury version uses fresh bread—you can also try using fruit bread.

Serves 4–6

5 tbsp butter, softened, plus extra
  for greasing
6 slices thick white bread
1/3 cup mixed dried fruit (golden
  raisins, currants, and raisins)
1 tbsp candied peel
3 large eggs
1 1/4 cups milk
2/3 cup heavy cream
1/4 cup superfine sugar
whole nutmeg, for grating
1 tbsp raw brown sugar

- Preheat the oven to 350°F/180°C. Grease an 8 x 10-inch/ 20 x 25-cm baking dish.

- Spread the butter over the slices of bread. Cut each slice of bread diagonally into quarters, then arrange half the bread overlapping in the prepared baking dish.

- Scatter half the mixed dried fruit and peel over the bread, cover with the remaining bread slices, and add the remaining fruit and peel.

- In a pitcher, beat the eggs well and stir in the milk, cream, and superfine sugar. Pour into the baking dish and let stand for 15 minutes to let the bread soak up some of the egg mixture.

- Tuck the dried fruit and peel under the bread slices so that they don't burn. Grate a little nutmeg over the top, then sprinkle over the brown sugar.

- Place the dish on a baking sheet and bake at the top of the preheated oven for 30–40 minutes, until just set and golden brown. Serve warm.

Apple Cake

Apples have been grown in Ireland for many centuries—legend has it that St Patrick himself planted an apple tree in an ancient settlement outside Armagh city. Today, Armagh County is known as "Orchard County" and celebrates its apples with festivals and apple blossom tours. This cake is a delicious way of using apples and can be served warm for dessert.

Serves 8

1 lb/450 g baking apples
1¼ cups self-rising flour
1 tsp ground cinnamon
pinch of salt
½ cup butter, plus extra for greasing
generous ½ cup superfine sugar
2 eggs
1–2 tbsp milk
confectioners' sugar, for dusting

Streusel Topping
generous ¾ cup self-rising flour
6 tbsp butter
scant ½ cup superfine sugar

❖ Preheat the oven to 350°F/180°C. Grease a 9-inch/23-cm round springform cake pan. To make the streusel topping, sift the flour into a bowl and rub in the butter using your fingertips until the mixture resembles coarse breadcrumbs. Stir in the superfine sugar and reserve.

❖ Peel, core, and thinly slice the apples. Sift the flour into a bowl with the cinnamon and salt. Place the butter and superfine sugar in a separate bowl and beat together until light and fluffy. Gradually beat in the eggs, adding a little of the flour mixture with the last addition of egg. Gently fold in half the remaining flour mixture, then fold in the rest with the milk.

❖ Spoon the batter into the prepared pan and smooth the surface. Cover with the sliced apples and sprinkle the streusel topping evenly over the top. Bake in the preheated oven for 1 hour, or until browned and firm to the touch. Let cool in the pan. Dust the cake with confectioners' sugar before serving.

Rhubarb Crumble

This comforting and homely dessert is incredibly simple to make—you can even make the crumble topping a day or so in advance and store it in the refrigerator until you are ready to use it. For an extra-crunchy topping, use raw brown sugar in place of the light brown sugar.

Serves 6

2 lb/900 g rhubarb
½ cup superfine sugar
grated rind and juice of
 1 orange
cream, yogurt, or custard,
 to serve

Crumble Topping
generous 1½ cups all-purpose flour
½ cup butter, diced and chilled
½ cup light brown sugar
1 tsp ground ginger

❧ Preheat the oven to 375°F/190°C.

❧ Cut the rhubarb into 1-inch/2.5-cm lengths and put in an ovenproof dish with the superfine sugar and orange rind and juice.

❧ To make the crumble topping, sift the flour into a bowl. Rub in the butter with your fingertips until the mixture resembles fine breadcrumbs. Stir in the brown sugar and ginger. Spread evenly over the fruit and press down lightly with a fork.

❧ Bake in the center of the preheated oven for 25–30 minutes, until the crumble is golden brown. Serve warm with cream, yogurt, or custard.

DOO LOUGH, COUNTY MAYO

Blackberry Soup with Buttermilk Custards

Although dried carrageen (Irish moss) would traditionally have been used as a thickening agent for custards and milk puddings, this recipe uses the more readily available gelatin. The sweet and inky blackberry soup and wobbly buttermilk custards are a sublime combination.

Serves 4

Buttermilk Custards
4 sheets gelatin
generous 1 cup buttermilk
generous 1 cup heavy cream
$1/4$ cup milk
$1/2$ cup superfine sugar

Blackberry Soup
1 lb/450 g blackberries
$1^1/4$ cups fruity red wine
scant $1/2$ cup water
$1/3$ cup superfine sugar, or to taste
2 star anise
4–5 tbsp blackberry liqueur (optional)

❖ To make the custards, put the gelatin in a small bowl, then cover with cold water and let soak for 5 minutes. Meanwhile, heat the buttermilk, cream, and milk together in a saucepan to just below boiling point. Add the sugar and stir until it has completely dissolved. Remove the gelatin from the soaking liquid and squeeze out any excess water. Add to the hot buttermilk mixture and stir until completely dissolved. Pour through a fine strainer and fill four dariole molds or individual ovenproof molds. Transfer to the refrigerator and chill for several hours, or overnight, until set.

❖ To make the blackberry soup, put the blackberries, wine, and water in a large saucepan with the sugar and star anise. Simmer very gently for 8–10 minutes, or until the sugar has dissolved and the mixture has a lovely anise scent. Remove from the heat and let cool. Once the mixture has cooled, remove and discard the star anise, then transfer to a food processor and blend until smooth. Pour through a fine strainer and stir in the liqueur, if using. Cover and chill in the refrigerator until ready to serve.

❖ To serve, divide the blackberry soup between four soup plates (rather than deep bowls) and place a buttermilk custard in the center of each.

Irish Cream Cheesecake

This is an unbaked cheesecake and although it contains no gelatin, its high chocolate content ensures that it sets perfectly. It is a luxurious dessert that is made even more special by the addition of Irish Cream, a popular liqueur made from Irish whiskey, coffee, and cream.

Serves 8

vegetable oil, for oiling
6 oz/175 g chocolate chip cookies
4 tbsp unsalted butter
sour cream and fresh strawberries,
  to serve

Filling

8 oz/225 g semisweet chocolate,
  broken into pieces
8 oz/225 g milk chocolate, broken
  into pieces
generous 1/4 cup superfine sugar
1 1/2 cups cream cheese
scant 2 cups heavy cream, lightly
  whipped
3 tbsp Irish Cream liqueur

❖ Line the bottom of an 8-inch/20-cm round springform cake pan with parchment paper and brush the sides with oil. Place the cookies in a plastic bag and crush with a rolling pin. Put the butter in a pan and heat gently until melted. Stir in the crushed cookies. Press into the bottom of the prepared cake pan and chill in the refrigerator for 1 hour.

❖ Put the semisweet and milk chocolate into a heatproof bowl set over a pan of gently simmering water until melted. Let cool. Put the sugar and cream cheese in a bowl and beat together until smooth, then fold in the cream. Fold the melted chocolate into the cream cheese mixture, then stir in the liqueur.

❖ Spoon into the cake pan and smooth the surface. Let chill in the refrigerator for 2 hours, or until quite firm. Transfer to a serving plate and cut into slices. Serve with sour cream and strawberries.

Irish Coffee

Irish coffee is a cocktail made with strong, hot coffee, Irish whiskey, and sugar, topped with thick cream. It is the perfect way to round off a meal or to ward off the night's chill. You'll need a steady hand to get the cream to float on top, but practice makes perfect!

Serves 1

2 measures Irish whiskey
1 tsp sugar, or more to taste
freshly made strong black coffee
2 measures heavy cream

❇ Put the whiskey into a warmed heatproof glass with sugar to taste. Pour in the coffee and stir until the sugar has completely dissolved.

❇ Pour the cream very slowly over the back of a spoon that is just touching the top of the coffee and the edge of the glass. Keep pouring until all the cream is added and has settled on the top.

❇ Do not stir—drink the coffee through the cream.

TORC WATERFALL, COUNTY KERRY

Black Velvet

This beer cocktail is made using equal measures of stout and white sparkling wine (traditionally Guinness and champagne). The different densities of the liquids mean that they should remain in separate layers, as in a pousse-café. For a Poor Man's Black Velvet, use hard cider instead of the wine, pouring it into the glass first and floating the stout on top.

Serves 1

stout, chilled
sparkling white wine, chilled

❖ Fill a tumbler halfway with stout, then very slowly pour in an equal quantity of wine over the back of a spoon that is just touching the top of the stout and the edge of the glass. This should prevent the drinks from mixing together too much and help to keep them in separate layers. Serve immediately.

BUNRATTY FOLK PARK, COUNTY CLARE

Index